LIFEWAYS

The Seminole

RAYMOND BIAL

BENCHMARK BOOKS

MARSHALL CAVENDISH
NEW YORK

SERIES CONSULTANT: JOHN BIERHORST

ACKNOWLEDGMENTS

This book would not have been possible without the help of many individuals and organizations that have dedicated themselves to understanding and preserving the traditions and beliefs of the Seminole. I am especially grateful to Mike "Skeet" Jones and all the staff at the Native Village at Hollywood, Florida, and the Ah-Ta-Thi-Ki Museum in Clewiston, Florida, for their generous assistance. I would also like to acknowledge the assistance of the National Archives, the Library of Congress, and the Philbrook Museum for furnishing several illustrations for *The Seminole*.

I would like to express my appreciation to my editor, Kate Nunn, and to Doug Sanders for their hard work and good humor in editing *The Seminole* and others in the *Lifeways* series from concept to finished book. I would also like to extend a hearty thanks to John Bierhorst who has diligently overseen each of the books in this series, thereby rescuing me from a number of embarrassing errors. As always, I would like to thank my wife, Linda, and my children Anna, Sarah, and Luke, for their encouragement and support of my work.

Benchmark Books
Marshall Cavendish Corporation
99 White Plains Road Tarrytown, New York 10591-9001
Text copyright © 2000 by Raymond Bial
Map copyright © 2000 by the Marshall Cavendish Corporation
Map by Rodica Prato

Library of Congress Cataloging-in-Publication Data
Bial, Raymond.
The Seminole / Raymond Bial.
p. cm.— (Lifeways)
Includes bibliographical references (p.) and index.
Summary: Discusses the history, culture, social structure, beliefs,
and customs of the Seminole people.
ISBN 0-7614-0862-2 (lib. bdg.)
1. Seminole Indians—History—Juvenile literature. 2. Seminole Indians—Social life and
customs—Juvenile literature. [1. Seminole Indians. 2. Indians of North America—Florida.]
I. Title. II. Series: Bial, Raymond. Lifeways.
E99.S28B47 2000
975.9"004973—dc21 98-50427
CIP AC

Cover photos: Raymond Bial

The photographs in this book are used by permission and through the courtesy of: The Philbrook Museum of Art, Tulsa, Oklahoma: 1, 16, 31, 32, 44, 51, 59, 63, 69, 71, 72, 117 Raymond Bial: 6, 8-9, 15, 21, 22, 24-25, 27, 34, 35, 36-37, 46, 47, 55, 56, 60, 66-67, 86, 90-91, 93(top & bottom), 94 (top & bottom), 101, 102-103. Smithsonian Institution, National Anthropological Archives: 12, 40, 82. Historical Museum of Southern Florida: neg. # 89-30, 28; neg. # 72-30, 43; neg. # 1985-73-2, 52; neg. # 16-30, 57. Library of Congress: 41, 79, 80-81, 85. National Archive: 48. Amon Carter Museum, Fort Worth, Texas: unknown artist, 39. *A Seminole Family*, ca. 1880-1890, albumen silver print, P1970.81.11, 74-75; after Charles Bird King, *Foke-Luste-Hajo. A Seminole*, 1842, lithograph, 1975.64.85, 109; after Charles Bird King, *Micanopy. A Seminole Chief*, 1838, lithograph, 1975.64.88, 113; after Charles Bird King, *Nea-Math-La, A Seminole Chief*, 1838, lithograph, 1975.74.73, 114.

This book is dedicated to
the proud Seminole people of
Florida and Oklahoma.

Contents

Author's Note

At the dawn of the twentieth century, Native Americans were thought to be a vanishing race. However, despite four hundred years of warfare, deprivation, and disease, American Indians have not gone away. Countless thousands have lost their lives, but over the course of this century the populations of native tribes have grown tremendously. Even as American Indians struggle to adapt to modern Western life, they have also kept the flame of their traditions alive—the language, religion, stories, and the everyday ways of life. An exhilarating renaissance in Native American culture is now sweeping the nation from coast to coast.

The Lifeways books depict the social and cultural life of the major nations, from the early history of native peoples in North America to their present-day struggles for survival and dignity. Historical and contemporary photographs of traditional subjects, as well as period illustrations, are blended throughout each book so that readers may gain a sense of family life in a tipi, a hogan, or a longhouse.

No single book can comprehensively portray the intricate and varied lifeways of an entire tribe, or nation. I only hope that young people will come away with a deeper appreciation for the rich tapestry of Indian culture—both then and now—and a keen desire to learn more about these first Americans.

1. Origins

According to the Seminole story of origin, which is traced back to their Creek ancestors, people and animals once lived in the sky. The earth was covered with water until the first soil was brought up from its depths.

"Crawfish and Eagle"

In the beginning there was no land. Only water covered the earth, and only the fish and the turtles could live there. All the people and animals made their home in the sky, which was very crowded. Finally, the Great Sky Council met and decided to look for new lands; they chose Eagle to be their leader in this quest.

"Let us send someone to Earth," Eagle suggested, "to see if there is soil from which we can make land."

Dove agreed to fly down. The council ordered him to stay no more than four days. He flew to every corner of the earth, but found only water. When he returned to the sky, he sadly reported that he could not find any land. Crawfish stepped forward and announced, "I will go down to Earth." The council allowed him to make the journey, but reminded him that he must return in four days. Slowly, Crawfish crept down to Earth and swam through the water, but he found no land. Finally, on the fourth and last day, he gathered all his strength and plunged deep to the bottom of the ocean. He was about to give up when he struck something. It was soft and squishy. "Mud!" Crawfish cried joyfully to himself.

On the evening of the fourth day, Crawfish returned to the Great Sky Council. Everyone thought that, like Dove, he had failed in his search for land. A hush fell over the people as Crawfish approached the fire. Standing on his hind legs, he thrust his claws upward. As he opened his claws, everyone could see the wet soil.

The Great Sky Council was delighted. Now, not only could the fish and turtles live on Earth, but all the animals could make a home there. Yet Eagle strode to the center of the fire and reminded everyone, "We cannot live on the lands as they are now—under the great waters. But I know a way to make better lands for us."

The council agreed, "The earth must be a dry place where we can live."

Eagle walked over to Crawfish and took the soggy soil from his claws. He rolled the soil in his powerful legs, round and round, until it was shaped into a vivid red ball. Grasping the ball in his talons, he spread his great wings and soared over the Great Sky Council.

With all his strength, he hurled the red ball toward the earth. The ball spun so rapidly that it looked like a shooting star. Exploding into the broad waters, which parted in waves, the ball spread red soil far and wide over the face of the earth.

However, these lands were still quite muddy, so Eagle flew over them and fanned his wings to dry them. The people and the animals then descended from the sky and made their homes on the earth, where they live to this very day.

THE FIRST NATIVE PEOPLES OF NORTH AMERICA ARRIVED MORE THAN 12,000 years ago, when much of the earth was covered with ice. At that time the seas were lower, and a land bridge connected Siberia and Alaska. Most likely, the people who crossed over from

*T*omochichi and his nephew posed for this mezzotint by John Faber. The portrait illustrates the traditional dress and body decoration of the Creeks who later became known as the Seminoles.

Siberia were pursuing wild animals, upon which they depended for food, clothing, and shelter. In time the people drifted southward, spreading throughout North America. Most of the people who settled in the Southeast spoke a group of related languages known as Muskogean. Among them one tribe, the ancestors of the Seminoles, spoke Muskogee. They moved into the forests of the present-day states of Alabama and Georgia. Settling along rivers, they hunted, fished, and gathered. Eventually, they cut down trees and cultivated the fertile land, raising corn, beans, and squash. While the men hunted, traded, and waged war, the women learned to make baskets and pottery, as well as clothing for their families.

As the population grew, these Muskogee people gathered in towns and developed a stable form of government under the leadership of chiefs known as *mikkos*. A league was created in which the mikkos from different towns came together and established laws for all the Muskogees. After explorers and traders of European descent encountered these people in the 1600s, they came to be known as Creeks, since they made their homes along rivers and streams. The Creeks began to trade with both the English colonists at Charleston in present-day South Carolina and the Spanish in Florida, as well as the French in New Orleans. However, in the early 1700s English settlers began to push into Creek lands. During the Yamasee War, the Creeks attacked settlements in the southern Carolinas in an effort to drive away the English. In 1716, fearing British retaliation, the Creeks living in present-day Georgia began to move south into the Spanish colony of Florida.

The Spanish welcomed the Creeks as a buffer against the British and encouraged them to settle in the former homeland of the Timucua and the Apalachee in the northern part of the peninsula. Many of these Lower Creeks, as they were then known, came in small bands and established a way of life based on hunting, gathering, and farming. Some groups of Lower Creeks also moved to Florida to get away from the Upper Creeks who had come to dominate their lives. However, because of their smaller numbers, they did not rebuild their town societies. Early in the eighteenth century, other Muskogean-speaking peoples from Georgia and Alabama, including the Choctaws, whose lives had similarly been disrupted by British expansion in the Southeast, also fled to the Spanish colony. They were joined by escaped African-American slaves who sought better lives as free people deep in the forests, wetlands, and slow-flowing rivers of Florida.

At the time these newcomers arrived, Florida was also home to remnants of tribes who had been living there for at least 12,000 years. When the Spanish came to Florida in 1513, there were 100,000 aboriginal people in Florida, largely from three major tribes—Calusa, Timucua, and Apalachee—along with about fifty smaller bands. However, during the 1600s most of these early Floridians succumbed to disease brought by the Europeans or were killed in warfare with the Spanish. Others were nearly annihilated by 1715, when British soldiers from the Carolinas invaded

The remote stretches of water and occasional woods in the Everglades, or "River of Grass," made an excellent hideout for Seminoles and runaway slaves. They easily avoided the Spanish, as well as the English and later the American settlers.

Spanish Florida in a series of raids. The few remaining Florida natives were assimilated into the Spanish population or intermarried with the Creeks and other Muskogean-speaking peoples when they moved into the region.

In the 1770s the Native American peoples of Florida, now largely of Creek descent, became known as the Seminole—perhaps from a mispronunciation of the Spanish *cimarrone*, which means "wild." The Spanish referred to them as Cimarrones (Wild People,

In the watercolor painting entitled The Unconquered Ones, *artist Jerome Tiger shows Seminole warriors keeping a lookout for their pursuers deep in the backwaters of the Everglades.*

or Runaways) because they would not allow themselves to be dominated. However, some scholars think the word *Seminole* may have come from *Simanoli*, the word the early Creeks used to refer to themselves. After moving into Florida, the Creeks began to call themselves *Ikaninuksalgi*, meaning "people on the point of the land."

Many African-American slaves, including those who joined the Seminoles, were skilled artisans and farmers, as well as excellent warriors. Not only did the fugitives share a thirst for freedom with the Seminoles, they significantly enriched native culture. They intermarried and assumed key leadership positions with full rights as tribal members. The former slaves quickly adapted to semitropical Florida, where the climate was similar to their African homeland. They also found a relatively safe haven in the remote and inaccessible backwaters of Florida, which made it difficult, often impossible, for slaveholders to track and capture them. Because these African Americans often spoke several languages, including English, Spanish, and Muskogee, they were invaluable as guides and advisers. Seminole chief Micanopy had an African-American wife, for instance, and Abraham, an influential African American, served as his able companion and confidant during hostilities with the Americans.

As white settlers pushed into the Florida peninsula, the Seminoles were driven farther south. However, the Seminoles resisted and conflicts escalated in the early 1800s, leading to three long and bitter Seminole Wars. During the 1830s and 1840s, the southern tribes, including the Seminoles, were forced to relinquish their lands and move to Oklahoma. At least three thousand Seminoles were removed to Indian Territory in the present state of Oklahoma. The Seminoles and other southern tribes eventually reestablished their governments in Oklahoma. Today, many Cherokees, Choctaws, Creeks, Chickasaws, and Seminoles follow their traditional beliefs. Others, while maintaining their tribal membership, have become integrated into the mainstream of American life.

Today, Seminole lands are scattered across south Florida. In addition to the Big Cypress, Hollywood, and Miccosukee Reservations, there are tribal centers at Tampa, Fort Pierce, and Immokalee.

Several thousand Seminoles, mostly small farmers, now live in Oklahoma. However, several hundred Seminoles resisted all attempts to remove them. Remaining in Florida, they continued to live as their ancestors did in thatched dwellings called *chickees*, meaning "homes," built on stilts above the damp, often flooded, ground of the marshes and swamps. Their descendants now make their homes on reservations near Lake Okeechobee and in the Everglades, or "River of Grass," and Big Cypress Swamp. They are noted for their colorful dress adapted from Spanish styles of the 1700s, but are most proud of their reputation as the Unconquered People, as they call themselves today.

The People and the Land

For hundreds of years, the Creek ancestors of the Seminoles lived in the hills and valleys of the Southeast, mostly clustered in towns along rivers and streams. When they were driven from their homes, they settled in the pine forests of upland Florida in the northern part of the state and along the coastal plain. Before long, however, they were forced to move again, this time seeking refuge in the swampy land of south Florida, where they live today.

This vast wetland encompasses nearly four thousand square miles in the southern part of Florida. Reaching from Lake Okeechobee, the region includes much of the southern peninsula from present-day Miami to the Gulf of Mexico. In the northern Everglades, grasslands rise from the shallow waters—saw grass grows as tall as ten feet in some places. There are also cypress swamps, where groves of trees are rooted in the shaded water. Bald cypress, bays, custard apples, wax myrtles, and willows anchor themselves on clumps of slightly higher ground called hammocks, or tree islands. Toward its southern edge, the Everglades blends with saltwater marshes and mangrove swamps on the coast. Okeechobee is the largest lake in the state and, after Lake Michigan, the largest body of freshwater entirely within the United States. Gurgling springs and tens of thousands of shallow lakes also glimmer through the thick grasses swaying in the breeze.

The Everglades bursts with wildlife—fish, alligators, snakes, turtles, deer, and panthers. Herons, pelicans, and many other graceful birds wade at the edge of the water or glide over the tree-tops. Of the varied and abundant creatures, the toothy alligator is the best known. With powerful, bone-crushing jaws, the long-tailed, large-jawed reptile silently eases through the water to ambush its prey—fish, small animals, and an occasional dog. Seminole men once hunted the reptiles for their meat and hides, but since the 1920s they have entertained tourists wrestling the scaly gators with their thrashing tails and snapping jaws.

For the better part of the 1800s the Seminoles artfully eluded soldiers who tried to flush them from the dense green trees and grass-covered swamps of the Everglades. Living off the land and the water, the people built temporary camps. If discovered, they simply vanished into the woods or glided in dugouts over the mir-rorlike waters by the light of the pale moon. When they found

Much of the Everglades is dotted with hammocks, or small islands, and groves of cypress trees. These trees grow from a wide base right out of the water.

another secluded place, they set up another camp. While they fished and hunted and farmed small garden patches on the hammocks, their pursuers slogged, hot and hungry, through the muck, or got lost in the thick foliage.

To this day, long after the wars, the Seminole have remained close to the land—and to its water. If either of these elements is damaged, so too are the people. In 1906, they were very concerned when the state of Florida began to drain large parts of the Everglades so the fertile muck could be farmed. Canals were dredged from Lake Okeechobee southeastward to the ocean. Sugar cane and vegetables grew well, but the dry ground caught fire easily. Also, salt water seeped from the ocean into this freshwater habitat. In 1947, to help save this remarkable wetland, the United States set aside its southwestern part as the Everglades National Park.

A*lligators are the best-known and most dangerous creatures of the Everglades. The Seminoles hunted them, but had to make sure they didn't become the hunted, as the gators cruised through the water, eyes just above the surface.*

However, Florida's population continued to grow after World War II, and the Everglades has been further threatened—land was lost to urban sprawl on the eastern edge and water levels dropped. During the 1960s, the U.S. Army Corps of Engineers built a system of dams that turned the Kissimmee River into a channel. Because the Kissimmee is the primary source of freshwater for Lake Okeechobee and the wetlands to the south, water was drained away from the Everglades. The loss of water has drastically changed the environment, and much of the wildlife has died.

Since 1983, the federal government has taken steps to protect what is left of the Everglades and has attempted to correct some of the previous damage. The Seminoles have also embarked upon a number of environmental programs to save the wetlands and woods that are their home. Along with the Environmental Protection Agency, they monitor the level and quality of water in the Everglades. As part of the Seminole Land Claims Settlement Act of 1987, the tribe agreed to transfer land and water rights for a portion of the Big Cypress Swamp to the state's program for Everglades restoration. The Seminoles no longer live and hunt on these lands and waters. Their reservations are now located on the eastern, northern, and western fringes of the Everglades. Of the original Seminole inhabitants, about two hundred reside in the southern part of the park. These Independents, as they are known, live along the Tamiami Trail, or U.S. Highway 41, which winds across the state from Miami to the Gulf Coast. Today, as in the past, the Everglades is their home, and it is critically important to all the Seminoles to save the land for future generations.

2. Florida Home

With a raised platform to keep people and belongings above floodwaters and with open sides to catch the breezes on hot and humid summer days, the chickee is an ideal home for life in the swamp.

THROUGHOUT THE 1700s CREEKS CONTINUED TO MOVE TO NORTH AND central Florida, where they established towns along the rivers. The land on which they settled was fertile and teeming with wildlife. One of the largest and best-known settlements was Cuscowilla, which had around thirty family dwellings. Skillful and hardworking, the Seminoles, as they came to be called, tended crops and raised livestock. They also hunted, fished, and traded with the Spanish who governed Florida at the time. The Spanish wanted fish and furs, as well as bear oil, honey, and other natural products, while the Seminoles had developed a taste for sugar, coffee, and tobacco. They also sought the cloth and cooking utensils the Spanish could provide.

Like other Creek peoples, the Seminole lived in log houses plastered with red clay. They grouped these houses around a square and a main building. Most families had two houses—one for storage and another for cooking meals during the day and sleeping at night. Some of the houses had two stories, with the sleeping quarters upstairs, and a porch from which the husband greeted visitors. Each family also had its own garden in which they raised corn, beans, melons, squash, and other vegetables for themselves. Each family also contributed to the public stores of food, fed visitors to the town, including runaway slaves, and helped the less fortunate members of the tribe. There were large community fields as well, in which everyone helped in planting, cultivating, and harvesting crops. These fields were fenced to keep domestic livestock and wild animals from devouring the corn and other vegetables.

Even the torrential downpours of semitropical Florida flowed down the chickee's steep thatched roofs, keeping inhabitants high and dry.

Town Society

The Creek ancestors of the Seminoles, when first encountered by Europeans, had been living on a land of woods and rivers for thousands of years. They had long since established a well-defined society, including an effective means of government. Nearly five hundred years ago, the Spanish observed that each town, whether large or small, had two different leaders—a peace chief, or mikko, and a war chief during times of conflict. In some towns, the position of peace chief was inherited. However, neither clan membership nor social status prevented this leader from

In colorful clothing with bold, distinctive designs, the men, women, and children of this village gathered outside their thatched-roof chickees in a photograph made by Claude C. Matlock in 1923.

being removed if he failed the people. Entrusted to seek the common good, the peace chief managed daily affairs and also served as religious leader in ceremonies. The peace chief listened to the people and learned of their needs, then took these concerns to the council.

Each town had a tribal council composed of the wisest and oldest men, who advised the peace chief. They shared responsibility for the welfare of the town. During times of conflict, they elected a man known for his bravery, skill in battle, and leadership as war chief. However, when the English encountered the Creeks, they completely disrupted their way of life. They demanded land, furs, and deerskins and attempted to force the people into military alliances against the Spanish and French. Warfare and disease brought widespread death and destruction. Strange diseases, including measles and smallpox, wiped out thousands of people who had no resistance. Fierce competition for land and resources among the Spanish, English, and French resulted in further deaths as well as the displacement of natives from the region. The social upheaval prevented them from ever returning to the town life they had known before.

Camps and Clans

Many Creeks remained in Georgia and Alabama until they were forcibly removed in the early 1800s to Oklahoma—where they live to the present day. Other Creeks, however, fled south to

Florida and became known as the Seminoles. Here, they no longer had enough people to establish towns. Instead, small bands lived in scattered camps. Eight to ten chickees were built on small islands of forested ground, or hammocks, slightly higher than the surrounding swamp.

Seminole society also became more strongly organized into clans of several closely related families. Each clan had its own story of origin. Family lineage was traced through the mother, who was responsible for preserving ancestral customs. A man might live in his wife's clan, but he remained a member of the clan into which he was born. If the last female in a clan died, the clan became extinct, or the "fire was put out," as the Seminoles said. Several historical clans, including Alligator, are now gone. Among the traditional clans were Panther, Wildcat, Bird, Otter, Wind, Snake, Wolf, and Town.

People were not allowed to marry members of their own clan. When a young couple married, the husband went to live in his mother-in-law's home. After a few years the couple might move into their own chickee if the husband could provide household goods, but the woman remained the head of the family. Their children were always considered members of her clan. Along with her brothers and other respected men of her clan, the mother was responsible for raising the children. Among the Seminoles, infidelity and divorce have always been quite rare.

Clan members tended to live together in a small cluster of chickees known as a *huti*, which referred to both the home place, the

*T*his 1962 watercolor is by Fred Beaver, an Oklahoma Creek artist best known for his pictures of Florida Seminole life. Two women cook together over a community fire in the foreground while two others grind corn in the distance

economic duties of providing food and clothing, and the social life. Women owned the home, livestock, and crops, while men followed the warpath and the hunting trails. Men and women built their chickee and worked in the fields together, but otherwise they had separate daily tasks. Men made tools and weapons while

In this 1966 watercolor by Jerome Tiger entitled Fish for Supper, *a man balances himself in a dugout as he throws his spear. The waters of the Everglades teemed with fish, many of which found their way into Seminole cooking pots.*

the women prepared meals, sewed clothing, and looked after the children. The women ran the household; the men governed the town and entertained visitors.

To this day, every Seminole is a member of his or her mother's clan. There are still many clans among the Seminole, including Panther, Bear, Deer, Bigtown, Bird, Snake, and Otter. Panther is the largest clan in Florida. Clan members are still not allowed to intermarry. A person must be at least one quarter Seminole to qualify as a tribal member.

Chickees

The traditional Seminole chickee consisted of a frame made of vertical palmetto or cypress logs and a sloping roof thatched with palmetto leaves, or fronds. The one-room building, about ten by sixteen feet, had no walls. Its open sides allowed the occasional breezes of steamy south Florida to flow through the chickee. Its floor was made by laying split palmetto logs flat side up and lashing them to upright logs with palmetto ropes. The platform raised the chickee about three feet aboveground to keep the family's belongings dry in the event of rising water. This style of building was first used by the Seminoles when they were pursued by American troops. They needed a basic shelter that could be easily put up and abandoned if they had to flee the soldiers.

Other native people in North and South America lived in similar dwellings, but the chickee frame lasted longer—about ten years—even in the warm, damp climate, and needed to be

With just living space and no walls, the chickee had little room for storage. However, goods could be safely tucked under the rafters, where they were not only out of the way but protected from the wind and water.

*C*hickees have proved to be well suited to the tropical climate of south
Florida. Many are used today as family homes and offices and as gathering
places in parks and tourist attractions.

rethatched only every five years or so. The chickee was so practi-
cal that it gave rise to a similar style of architecture now popular
throughout south Florida. Floors are now made of milled lumber
that is nailed instead of lashed together. Or the chickee may have
no floor—it may simply be erected over the bare ground. Today,
some chickees have electricity and bathrooms. Several members
of the Seminole Tribe of Florida now earn a livelihood construct-
ing chickees for use as commercial buildings and family homes.

3. Lifeways

The Seminole have long favored bold patterns and bright colors in a unique style of dress called patchwork.

TO THE SEMINOLES, ALL OF LIFE MAY BE VIEWED IN CYCLES—NOT ONLY the days, the seasons, and the years, but also the course of one's life and the generations. As people grow old and die, their children and grandchildren carry on the traditional lifeways. One of the most distinctive and graphic symbols of the Seminoles is the Wheel of Life. Composed of five colorful circles, each with a cross in the middle, the wheel represents the different phases of life and death. The inner red circle indicates good health. The blue circle symbolizes illness; the black circle represents death; yellow indicates the bones of a dead person; and white symbolizes the passage of time during which the bones are bleached. To this very day, the Seminoles deeply respect the cycles of life, just as they honor their ancestors and love their children.

Cycle of Life

Birth. Traditionally, a woman retired to a small "baby house" to give birth. Her newborn was bathed in the cold water of a nearby stream, and throughout their lives the Seminoles frequently "went to water" to purify themselves. The mother placed a little bag of fragrant herbs around the baby's neck to keep away evil spirits and to ensure good health. She remained in the baby house until her child was four months old. During this time, she prepared her own meals and avoided the men in the village, after which she returned to her family home. Her baby stayed in its own small hammock above the damp ground, safe from insects and snakes.

The mother often gently rocked the child back and forth as she worked in the chickee.

Childhood. Living deep in the Everglades, young children were taught to watch out for alligators, panthers, bears, poisonous snakes, and other dangerous creatures. During the Seminole Wars, they were also instructed to play quietly in the green leaves and grass so the soldiers would not be able to find their hidden camp. At night, children slept on furs or skins to acquire the qualities of the animal to whom it had belonged—boys on panther skins so they might be good hunters and girls on deerskins so they might become modest and gentle.

Parents were very fond of their children and often indulged them. Children usually respected and obeyed their parents. Occasionally, parents teased their children, but they rarely punished them. When discipline was necessary, the mother's brother might be called upon to scratch the arms or legs of an errant boy, but girls were never punished in this way. Siblings usually got along in a pleasant manner, although relations between brothers and sisters were somewhat formal. As brothers and sisters matured they might joke around with each other, but they generally avoided any physical contact.

At an early age, children began to work around the camp. Mothers taught their daughters all the skills needed to take care of a family. One of the mother's brothers or other adult males of

*S*porting several necklaces, Alice (Willie) Osceola, wife of William McKinley Osceola, posed with her daughter Mittie for this photograph taken by Frank A. Robinson around 1918.

F ramed by the lush, tropical foliage of the Everglades, a Seminole mother and her children pose on a wooden bridge that leads to their camp in the background.

her clan taught the sons to hunt, fish, and fight, as well as how to properly conduct themselves during ceremonies. When they were still quite young, boys learned to guide dugout canoes silently over the shallow water with long poles.

At twelve years of age, the boys were considered grown men with the same rights and responsibilities as other adult males. During the annual Green Corn Ceremony, boys between thirteen and fifteen years of age received a new name from their elders or from the medicine man that indicated their coming-of-age. Young girls learned to cook and sew, as well as to care for the babies and younger siblings. At age fourteen, they were skilled at these domestic tasks and ready to be married.

Marriage. Seminole women were always fond of jewelry, but when a woman wanted to find a husband, she started to drape herself in even more strings of beads and silver ornaments.

A person could marry only someone from a different clan. It was rare that a person married someone from the father's clan, although such marriages were not strictly forbidden.

When a couple wished to marry, they met with the leader of the woman's clan to seek permission. Often, however, a woman's family selected her husband for her. In fact, marriages helped to forge alliances between clans. So older relatives frequently arranged marriages for young people, sometimes without consulting the couple. The elders also considered the man's ability to be a good provider and the woman's skill in managing a house-

These people gathered for a joyful occasion—the wedding of a couple in their village. The photograph was taken by Claude C. Matlock in 1922.

hold. The couple had to agree to the marriage; no one had to accept a mate against his or her will. If no one in the clan objected, the couple was married during the Green Corn Ceremony or another festival.

Death. The medicine man usually attended to the burial of the dead. The body was placed on an open, raised platform under the shelter of a thatched roof in the swamp or woods. The deceased was surrounded by the possessions needed in the afterlife, all of which were first broken because people believed that was the only way these objects could pass into the spirit world. Exposed to the elements, the body quickly decomposed.

In this 1967 watercolor by Jerome Tiger entitled Death Scene, *a woman wraps herself in a shawl against the wind as she walks among the trees in mourning over the loss of a loved one.*

The family of the deceased mourned for four days. On the last morning they drank tea and washed with an herbal tonic made by the medicine man. If a married man died, his widow was required to mourn for a much longer period of time. She had to wear black and mourn for four moons. She also had to wait four years before she could marry again.

Living off the Land

As they withdrew into the Everglades, the Seminoles established camps, the center of which was cleared for a cooking and dining house with a large fire pit. Working together, the women cooked for everyone in the camp, as well as for visitors who stayed in this central building, which also served as a guesthouse. On the small, fertile hammocks they raised pumpkins, melons, and beans, but their most important crop was corn, the main ingredient in many tasty dishes, especially soups and breads. Soaking the hard kernels in wood ashes and water, women made hominy, which was included in many dishes, notably a soup known as *sofki*. Eating with a single sofki spoon, everyone shared this soup from a large bowl as it was passed from the men to the boys, to the women and the girls. Sofki, most often made with grits or roasted corn, is still a very popular soup today.

People also sustained themselves with wild game and fish. The Everglades teemed with wildlife, and hunters brought back alligator, deer, turkey, duck, rabbit, opossum, squirrel, and an occasional bear for the cooking pot. Skilled and knowledgeable out-

Here, alligator skins are drying in the sun. The Seminole ate the meat of the alligator, but sold the skins, which were used to make expensive purses and luggage.

doorsmen, the Seminole trapped small animals, such as rabbits and birds, or shot them with blowgun darts. They made the blowguns from long, straight cane stalks and the darts from sharp pieces of hardwoods.

For larger animals, such as deer, they fashioned stout bows from black locust, hickory, or other hardwoods. They twisted sinew or strips of deer hide to make the bowstring. These bows were so long and taut that only a strong man could draw back the bowstring. Men attached turkey feathers to long wooden stems to make the arrows, which were tipped with points made from fish bones. Later, when they had acquired kettles and pans, the men made points out of flattened pieces of brass and iron taken from the cooking vessels. They also traded for muzzleloading

Seminole men once hunted with handmade weapons. Today, they fashion wooden tomahawks and sell them to tourists along the highway.

guns, which soon replaced bows and arrows in both hunting and warfare.

In addition, the Seminoles gathered wild plants, nuts, and berries. From the underground stems of the arrowroot plant, or coontie, they made a kind of flour. Sometimes the coontie was sweetened with honey and made into a dessert much like pudding. Like other native peoples of the Southeast, the Seminoles did not have three regular meals a day. A pot of hot soup or sofki hung over the fire all day, and people ate whenever they were hungry. With the exception of sofki and fry bread, most traditional dishes are now made only on special occasions. Today Seminoles shop at grocery stores, call for pizza deliveries, and enjoy the same foods as other Americans.

The Seminole have always lived off the land as hunters, gatherers, and farmers. In this 1941 photograph, two women and a small boy are cooking down sugar cane to make a sweet syrup at the Seminole Indian Agency in Florida.

Pumpkin Soup

Here's a modern version of a favorite old recipe, adapted from *Seminole Indian Recipes*.

Ingredients:

2 cups chicken stock

1/2 green pepper, seeded and diced

1 large tomato

1 green onion

1 sprig parsley

1 teaspoon thyme

1 can pumpkin (16 ounce) or 2 cups cooked pumpkin cubes

1 tablespoon flour

2 tablespoons butter

1 cup of milk

1 teaspoon nutmeg

1 teaspoon sugar

Puree one cup chicken stock, pepper, tomato, onion, parsley and thyme in blender. Pour mixture into saucepan and simmer for five minutes.

Return mixture to the blender. Add pumpkin and flour. Blend on high speed until texture is smooth. Pour mixture into saucepan. Stir in remaining chicken stock and other ingredients. Heat to a low boil and cook for three minutes. Serve hot.

Clothing and Jewelry

Along with cooking, women were responsible for making all the clothes for their families, the styles of which changed dramatically after the arrival of the Europeans. When Spanish explorer Hernando de Soto first encountered the Creeks, they wore clothes made from animals skins and plant fibers—skirts for the women and breechcloths for the men—along with a kind of sleeveless cloak called a mantle. During the cold months they wore robes of marten or muskrat fur. They also painted or tattooed their faces and sometimes their bodies with dyes made from herbs and minerals. Women began to favor cloth, and their dress gradually blended elements of traditional and European styles. By the time the Creeks came to north Florida in the mid-1700s they had already abandoned their bark cloth and buckskin in favor of European-style garments. The lighter clothing was much better suited to the warm climate. Because of mosquitoes and other biting insects people favored clothes that covered much of their skin to the ankles, wrists, and necks.

Influenced by the Spanish colonists, women began to wear full, ankle-length skirts, gathered at the waist. These skirts often had a ruffle at the knee. Long-sleeved blouses, to which a cape was often attached, were trimmed with ruffles. Seminole men generally wore a simple long shirt tied with a leather or woven belt and decorated on the front. The shirt hung down over a loincloth or pants. Sometimes, they tied bright red or yellow scarves around their necks. For hats, they preferred a large turban, usually deco-

The long skirts of Seminole girls and women are often decorated with a band of brightly colored patterns. The designs were created over the past hundred years and are unique to the Seminoles of Florida. Painting by Fred Beaver.

rated with beads or stones. During cold weather or jaunts into town, men might also don a brightly colored coat, or "long shirt," adorned with ruffles. On special occasions they wore handwoven, intricately decorated sashes across their chests. People usually went barefoot, but in northern Florida they wore leather moccasins and leggings during cold weather.

Cotton procured from trading posts was the most common fabric used for making clothes. As for patterns, calico was the favorite, but people also wore garments made with stripes, solids, and occasionally plaid. Sometimes, cloth patterns were sewn onto the clothing. This became a popular technique for decorating

The variety of original designs in Seminole dress is well represented by the skirts of these women who gathered at the Musa Isle village for this photograph taken by Florence L. Randall in 1930.

dresses and shirts. Called patchwork, this uniquely Seminole style first consisted of blocks or bars of different colors, often in a sawtooth pattern, appliquéd onto the garment. As early as 1880, treadle sewing machines had appeared in many Seminole camps, and by 1892, it seemed that nearly every chickee had one. Around 1900, women began to sew a cloth waistband as a kind of belt in men's shirts—these became known as "Seminole jackets." At the same time, ruffles in women's blouses spread until they covered the blouse to the wrists and to the waist. Both of these styles have become a distinctive part of Seminole dress, along with the horizontal stripes of bright, contrasting color that are often sewn into garments.

For most of this century, visitors to south Florida have been highly impressed by the colors and bold designs of Seminole clothing. The most noted pattern consists of the striking bands of cloth, or patchwork. Often considered traditional dress, patchwork did not really come into fashion until about 1920. About this time, the designs became increasingly striking and complex, and Seminole sewing began to blossom into an art form that is passed down from mother to daughter. Patchwork has not only allowed women to earn additional income, but it has provided them with a creative outlet and a welcome break from the everyday chores of the camp.

Women have long adorned themselves with delicate jewelry. Early on, they wove shell beads into clothing. Colorful seeds were embroidered on woolen cloth to make pouches for pipes and tobacco, as well as other ceremonial objects. Women came to favor necklaces of strung beads. After contact with Europeans, colored glass beads came to replace shells and seeds. Women loved to drape many strings of brightly colored beads around their necks—sometimes as many as two hundred strands weighing fifteen to twenty pounds. They seldom removed the strands, even when they slept at night. They might also don silver necklaces made from Spanish or American coins pounded into thin wafers. They adorned themselves with rings and occasionally earrings as well. According to legend, a baby received her first necklace at birth and another strand every year until she reached middle age. Then a necklace was removed each year, until the old woman went to her grave with only the first necklace given to her at birth. Men often wore earrings of silver, brass, or glass beads, and occasionally, they pierced their noses. Seminole fashion reached a peak from the 1930s through the 1940s. Today, women sew beads into belts, headbands, and bracelets and still love to wear strands of brightly colored glass beads.

Handicrafts

Among their many labors, women made pottery, first coiling, then shaping the clay by hand. They cooked food in these pots, until iron and copper kettles became available. They also made storage vessels and bowls for holding food. The men fashioned clay pipe bowls with stems of hollow reeds or canes. The women

Women made lovely pottery. After firing the clay to harden it, they decorated it with pictures. Today, people still make the traditional pots and bowls, but mostly for sale to tourists.

Women wove baskets from palmetto leaves and other plant fibers, such as sweet grass and pine needles, to store their belongings. Today, sweet grass baskets, in particular, are sold as souvenirs.

hollowed out dried gourds for bowls, cups, and ladles. They also carved wooden spoons and cups, as well as mortars and pestles.

Women wove baskets and mats from split cane, which was readily available. As the Seminoles moved into south Florida, they began to weave the fibers of palmetto stalks into storage baskets. Sweet grass baskets have been made by the Seminoles for over sixty years. The sweet grass is picked by hand at high, fairly dry areas in the Everglades basin, thoroughly washed, and laid in the sun until dried. Using palmetto fiber as a base, women form baskets in many different shapes by weaving the sweet grass into coils that are held together with colorful thread.

Dugout Canoes

Unlike the Plains Indians, the Seminoles rarely rode horses. Instead, when they lived in northern Florida they traveled and hunted on foot, by oxcart, and occasionally on horseback. They established an extensive network of trails for hunting, trading, and visiting other towns. After moving into the swamps of southern Florida, however, they found themselves in a world of water. Here, boats were essential, and they quickly adopted the gracefully shaped dugout canoe as a primary means of transportation.

First they selected logs, preferably from cypress trees, which varied in length from twelve to thirty feet. They peeled the bark,

After carving their dugouts, men often decorated the surface. In this photograph made by Claude C. Matlock in the 1920s, three men demonstrate the traditional way in which they painted their canoes.

then hollowed out the trunk by placing burning embers on top. After the embers had burned down, they scraped the charred wood with steel blades or shells. The men worked patiently, repeatedly burning and scraping away the wood and shaping the sides and both ends, leaving a high seat at the stern, or rear. By the time the dugout was finished, the wood was perfectly seasoned.

Standing on the seat, a poler could easily look over the tall saw grass that blankets much of the Everglades. Although cypress is fairly lightweight, the canoes weighed between two and three hundred pounds. But with their flat bottoms and point rising in the front, they floated high in the water. The Seminoles often decorated the bows of their dugouts with elaborate designs representing their families.

Although men might make dugouts of different kinds of wood, cypress was preferred because it never rotted. Cypress dugouts were passed down from father to son over several generations. Today, the art of boatbuilding has nearly been lost. Automobiles and airboats have replaced the dugouts of the past.

Trading and Tourism

From the time they came to Florida, the Seminoles remained largely self-reliant, providing themselves with all the necessities of food, clothing, and shelter. Yet they also traded for some special items with other tribes and with the settlers, especially the

In this 1948 watercolor by Fred Beaver entitled Alligator Hunt, *three men poling in their dugout have caught an alligator. While one man stands over the alligator, the other clamps the reptile's jaws together.*

Spanish who had such a pervasive influence in Florida. Venturing to trading posts at the edge of the Everglades, the Seminoles swapped deerskins, alligator hides, fur, dried fish, and the plumes of egrets and other tropical birds for coffee, tobacco, and liquor, as well as guns, knives, pots, pans, and other household items. They also acquired the cloth they used to make their brightly colored garments.

Seminole dolls represent the many striking dress styles that women have created over the past hundred years. Each of these dolls is typically Seminole, yet each wears a dress of a different pattern.

Usually only the men made this journey to the trading posts, where they picked up a little English. Even if the women came along, they always held back and so never learned much English. Because of their isolation from Western culture, the women over time became pivotal in preserving Seminole language and traditional culture. By the 1870s the Seminoles were traveling by dugout or oxcart to Fort Myers and Miami. Fashion designers and milliners began to rely on their bird feathers and alligator hides for making hats and leather goods. A few Seminole hunters and trappers earned a living by harvesting wildlife. In 1905, however, the United States began to drain the Everglades, which led to a shocking decline in wildlife, and pushed the Seminoles into a deepening poverty.

In 1914, a resort owner named Henry Coppinger opened the first "Indian Village" in Florida as a tourist attraction. Soon other supposedly authentic villages were established in the southern part of the state. Whole families lived in these settlements modeled after camps perched on hammocks in the Everglades. On display to visitors, men, women, and children reenacted the daily routines of traditional Seminole life. A few people enjoyed living this way, but most felt demeaned—they wished to be far away from gawking tourists. Yet tourists paid to watch the men wrestle alligators and the women weave sweet grass baskets. Although alligator wrestling was never a traditional sport among the Seminoles, grappling with gators enabled men to earn a little income. At these villages and other roadside attractions, women

made and sold baskets, clothing, and other crafts, notably palmetto dolls. Made from palmetto husks stuffed with cotton, and
dressed in small garments with striking patterns, the dolls are not
just toys or souvenirs. They accurately portray the clothing and
hairstyle of traditional Seminole men and women. Palmetto dolls
are still the most popular item offered for sale at festivals and
other gatherings.

Games and Storytelling

When they were not busy tending crops or hunting in the
swamps, people enjoyed many games. *Chunkey* was a favorite of
the Seminoles and other peoples of the Southeast. Men and
women played this game together. The object was to hit a cow's
skull or a carved wooden fish at the top of a high pole with a ball.
Contestants were awarded four points if they struck the object
and two points if the ball hit within five to ten feet.

Another very popular game was stickball, which evolved into
the lacrosse of today. Men competed fiercely in this game, kicking,
hitting, and tackling as they battled over a small ball made with a
deerskin. This game helped men to strengthen themselves in
preparation for war.

People also entertained themselves and learned about their
history and traditions through stories. Late at night around the
campfires, safely tucked inside their mosquito nets, Seminole children enjoyed stories told by the old people of their town. Never

*T*his 1951 watercolor by Fred Beaver entitled Sing Ceremony—Eve of Creek Stickball Game *depicts the celebration that preceded the match. This popular game helped men to prepare themselves for the rigors of war.*

written down, the stories have been passed down over the generations, so whoever listens must remember and retell the stories as accurately as possible. The storyteller thus carries a great deal of responsibility, and even today the best storytellers are highly respected.

These beloved stories involve the mischievous Rabbit, the Corn Mother, the Deer Girl, and virtually every creature of the Everglades. The stories help to teach young and old about living in harmony with nature and each other. They explain the mysteries of the universe, as well as the beliefs and customs of the Seminole.

"Rabbit the Trickster"

Here is a version of a popular tale about a furry rascal who often appears in Seminole stories:

Rabbit was not only lazy, he was always causing trouble. Fed up with the many tricks he played on the people, the town council met and decided to do away with Rabbit once and for all. The men skillfully trapped the furry-tailed trickster and tied him up in a bag while they debated how best to get rid of him. Some members of the council wanted to throw him into the river; others wished to burn him in the fire. As the sun descended over the trees, they decided to toss him in the fire at the break of dawn the very next morning.

That night Wolf, who roams the woods after dark, stumbled upon Rabbit bound up in the sack.

"Is that you, Brother Wolf?" asked Rabbit.

"Why yes," answered Wolf. "Why are you tied up in that bag?"

Rabbit suddenly thought of a way he might escape from the bag, if only he could trick Wolf. He sighed, "They caught me and told me I must eat four tender little boys. But I don't eat people! I only nibble green grass and leaves. Yet if I don't devour those boys, they will throw me in the fire." Rabbit began to cry his heart out. "What am I going to do, Brother Wolf?"

Wolf, who was very fond of toothsome young children, licked his chops. "I will take your place. Let me get into that bag and I will eat those boys for you."

"What a wonderful idea!" cried Rabbit. "Wolf, you are so clever."

Wolf untied the bag, and Rabbit sprang out. He helped Wolf into the bag, which he knotted tightly, before hopping quickly away.

The next morning the council went to throw Rabbit into the fire. The bag seemed heavier, but they were so eager to be rid of him that they did not bother to look inside. Wolf's mouth watered. He couldn't wait to gobble up those little boys, but then he heard a Seminole man say, "Throw him in the fire." As he flew through the air, Wolf knew something was wrong—there were no children and it was getting awfully hot and smoky inside the bag.

Wolf began to howl in pain. Luckily, a hole burned in the side of the bag before he could be consumed by the flames. Wolf leaped out and ran away. Fortunately, his hide was not burned, but his fur was singed. Once again Rabbit had outsmarted the people—and Wolf. "I'll chase that Rabbit forever," growled Wolf as he vanished into the forest. "And when I catch him, I'll eat him." Since that time Wolf has relentlessly pursued Rabbit, who has become his favorite food. And, even to this day, Wolf's fur is scorched brown and burned black from the council fire.

4.Beliefs

The Seminoles believed that spirits inhabited everything, living and nonliving. They saw their lives as passing through the cycle of the seasons and the generations, and depicted their faith in a variety of signs and symbols.

THE SEMINOLES BELIEVE THAT SPIRITS DWELL IN ALL THINGS, NOT ONLY in plants and animals but in the earth itself, as well as the sun, the moon, and the stars. There are spirits in fire, water, and other elements. The Preserver of Breath is the greatest of the divine beings, and the Fire Spirit carries messages for him. Thunder, the god of war, brings the rain while Corn Mother watches over the gardens and fields. There are other supernatural creatures, ranging from terrifying water monsters to the Little People. Water monsters wrap themselves around their victims and drag them downward until they drown in the murky swamp. The mischievous Little People play tricks on the Seminoles, but they are also kind enough to help lost children find their way home.

Medicine

To the Seminole, body and soul are not separate; medicine and religion are the same. Medicine men have traditionally played a vital healing role—both spiritual and physical—in the lives of the Seminoles. Treating a variety of illnesses, elders and occasionally gifted young people used roots, herbs, animal parts, and other sacred cures from their medicine bundles as they chanted over the patient to the accompaniment of drums, bells, and rattles. Medicine men sometimes interpreted dreams as well. They also brought good luck, protected people from danger, and helped them to make good decisions. When needed, they prayed for good weather. It was a great honor to become a medicine man. Only a few boys were selected and they had to study diligently,

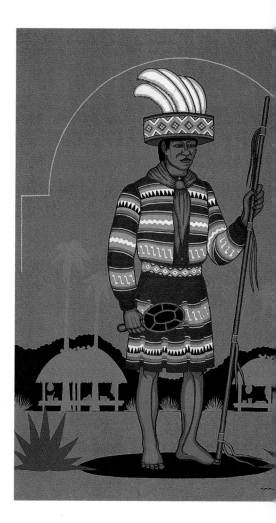

In this 1971 watercolor by Fred Beaver entitled Seminole Medicine Man, *this honored individual stands with staff and turtle shell rattle in hand. The medicine man treated illnesses and injuries of both the body and the soul.*

learning to gather plants and prepare herbal cures. However, before they could become medicine men, they had to study for at least seven years and sometimes as long as twenty. Even an experienced practitioner continued to learn new rituals and remedies for the rest of his life.

Today, most Seminoles go to medical doctors as well as to medicine men for diagnosis and treatment of sickness and injuries. Early missionaries zealously tried to convert the

Seminoles to Christianity with little consideration of the damage to native culture. Today most Seminoles have become Christians, but some people living in isolated areas follow the old ways, and most Seminoles continue to respect and follow their spiritual leaders.

Green Corn Ceremony

The Seminoles held many rituals over the course of the year in which they expressed their gratitude for good weather, abundant game, and bountiful harvests through chants, songs, and dances. The Green Corn Ceremony, or Busk, was the most important event. In the old days people came together in late June or early July to celebrate the first ripe corn of the season. This time was also considered the beginning of the new year. The actual date of the Green Corn Ceremony, which was held for four to eight days, was decided by the medicine man and his helpers.

The festival was also a time of healing, fasting, and spiritual cleansing. People drank a mysterious black liquid brewed from various leaves to purge themselves of ills. This beverage was also used to strengthen the warriors, who drank nothing else during this time. Boys and men ritually scratched themselves with needles. During the Green Corn Ceremony, young children learned about their religion. Couples were married, and occasionally a divorce was granted. Court Day, a practice from the old government, was held, and crimes against people were judged and appropriate punishments handed down. People who wished to

In this 1953 watercolor by Fred Beaver entitled Creek Baskita Corn Ceremony, *people have gathered on the dance ground. To this day, the Seminole hold this important annual ceremony.*

rid themselves of sin and sickness sought to begin life afresh. During this time of renewal, broken pottery was replaced and new patchwork clothes were worn. People played games during this festival as well, notably stickball. They also feasted, danced, and sang to the accompaniment of turtle shell rattles and water drums.

The person at the center the Green Corn Ceremony was the medicine man, who oversaw all the events. Held in very high esteem among the Seminoles, the medicine man carried within himself the entire history of his people—the stories, the rituals, and the beliefs. During the Green Corn Ceremony, he brought his medicine bundle out of hiding. Filled with bits of animal bones, feathers, horns, and herbs, the deerskin pouch was considered the medicine man's most valued means of healing people. He prayed that he would handle the medicine bundle properly during the ceremony and throughout the coming year.

Over the years, as they warred with English colonists and American soldiers, the Seminoles refused to abandon their ancient traditions. When the Seminole way of life was threatened,

In this 1949 watercolor by Fred Beaver entitled Creek Women's Ribbon Dance, *women dance in a line, as Seminoles in Florida and Oklahoma now do in the stomp dance.*

medicine men became even more important as the keepers of the cultural flame. High-ranking warriors not only protected the camp in battle but guarded the sacred traditions during peaceful times. After the tribe had been scattered by conflict with the Spanish and English and later the American soldiers, the Green Corn Ceremony helped to strengthen the clans and reaffirm their members' commitment to each other. In this ceremony, clan members remembered the source of strength and wisdom that had nourished them for countless generations. This long tradition of independence and belief in themselves carried the Seminoles through their many battles with American forces in Florida and has helped them to make a better life for themselves today.

Like their ancestors, the Seminoles of today gather each year for the Green Corn Ceremony to honor their traditions and to enjoy themselves. Seminoles still take part in the dance for purification and manhood ceremonies. Tribal disputes may also be resolved during this time. Men and women separate into "camps" according to their clans. Few non-Indians are permitted at Green Corn Ceremonies, which are held at undisclosed locations every spring. The gathering includes hours of "stomp dancing," in which people move single file in a methodical, weaving line behind a chanting medicine man. The string of male dancers responds to each of the chanter's exhortations, while women dancers quietly shuffle forward with shakers tied to their legs. Groups of stomp dancers occasionally appear at public events, demonstrating the dances of the fire ant, the crow, and the catfish.

5. Changing World

The Seminole Wars were all-out guerilla campaigns in which entire families fought for their survival. In this early photograph, a Seminole man, holding his rifle, poses with his wife and children.

DISPUTES WITH SETTLERS IN FLORIDA WERE INCREASING AT THE DAWN OF the nineteenth century. The settlers coveted Seminole land and also wanted their former slaves returned to them. In 1817, the first of three wars broke out between the Seminoles and the United States. General Andrew Jackson, a merciless Indian fighter, invaded Florida when Spain could not control the Seminoles. Jackson spent nearly two decades trying to resolve the Indian "problem" by eliminating the native peoples of the Southeast, including the Seminoles, through removal or killing. After he became president, the United States government continued this policy of destroying the Seminoles in body and spirit by waging three aggressive guerrilla-style campaigns that became known as the Seminole Wars. This ongoing conflict, which spanned a period of forty-two years, resulted in at least four broken treaties. Along with Old Hickory, as Jackson was known, an impressive list of military leaders attempted to remove the Seminoles. Edmund Gaines, Zachary Taylor, Duncan Clinch, Winfield Scott, Robert Call, and Alexander Macomb were among the leaders of the failed forty-year war to conquer the Seminoles.

The Seminole Wars

Throughout the colonial period, particularly during the American Revolution, African Americans took advantage of conflict—first between the Spanish and the English, then, during the American Revolution, between the Americans and the English—to escape from slavery. Many sought and received haven among the Seminoles. Spain, which first claimed Florida, refused to return the escapees to their irate owners in Georgia. The former slaves settled with the Seminoles, intermarried, and established themselves as farmers and tribal leaders.

During the War of 1812 the British, having taken over Florida, rebuilt an old Spanish fort approximately sixty miles from the border with the United States. Seminoles and runaway slaves were recruited to man the fort. They were soon making raids into Georgia, and their base became a major irritant to Georgia slaveholders. In 1816, American troops under Colonel Edmund Gaines attacked and destroyed the fort. In 1817, General Andrew Jackson started the First Seminole War when he led a second expedition of three thousand soldiers into Florida to attack a small group of Seminoles. Along with the Creeks, these Seminoles had been raiding white homesteads in Georgia. Jackson also sought to recapture runaway slaves. He destroyed many Seminole villages, scattering their inhabitants and eventually forcing the Spanish to sell Florida to the United States in 1819.

As the United States expanded westward, government officials also looked south to Florida where the Seminoles had established prosperous farms, citrus groves, and cattle ranches. At the time nearly five thousand Seminoles were living in small villages in the new American territory, along with about eight hundred African Americans. Their log houses, exposed in clearings, were vulnerable to attack. With an eye on Seminole land, settlers often provoked the native peoples into skirmishes and battles. In 1823, the Seminoles were forced to sign the Treaty of Moultrie Creek, which officially ended the First Seminole War. In this treaty, they surrendered most of their land. However, settlers still complained, because after the treaty as many as a hundred of their slaves had run away to find sanctuary. The African-American presence among the Seminole was a major reason that the removal of the Seminoles was sought, as they inspired other slaves to escape from plantations in Georgia and elsewhere.

In 1824 a capital city for Florida was established at Tallahassee. Around the city, in the fertile region between the Apalachicola and the Suwannee Rivers, the plantation system took root and flourished. Competition for this highly profitable land led to further efforts to relocate the Seminoles. With the passage of the Indian Removal Act in 1830, the United States attempted to systematically move all the Native Americans of the Southeast, including the Seminoles, to Indian Territory, in what is now Oklahoma. The Seminoles and runaway slaves refused to be relocated. In 1832, confronted by a flood of settlers and soldiers, many reluctantly agreed to migrate west of the Mississippi, yet a number of valiant warriors fought all efforts to remove them.

This resistance sparked the Second Seminole War. Legendary leader Osceola, joined by Chief Micanopy and several hundred warriors—including about a hundred African Americans—decided to fight any attempts to force them from their homeland. Osceola, who was also known as William Powell, punished anyone who cooperated with the whites and masterminded several battles

Osceola became a great Seminole leader. He skillfully and bravely guided his warriors in a number of battles against American soldiers, until his
capture on October 20, 1837.

Massacre of the Whites by the

Newspapers depicted the Second Seminole War as an uprising in which natives and escaped slaves massacred whites. In truth, the Seminoles were fighting to keep settlers from taking their homeland.

against five generals. Although he lacked the lineage of great chiefs, such as Micanopy and Jumper, the handsome, elegantly dressed warrior spoke defiantly. Hostilities began on December 28, 1835, when a band of Seminoles ambushed and killed Major Francis Dade and all but three of a 108-man regiment north of Tampa. In a separate attack, Osceola killed Indian agent Wiley

Thompson. After defeating United States military forces in early battles, Osceola was captured on October 21, 1837, when deceived by troops who agreed to speak with him under a flag of truce. Although Osceola died in prison in Charleston, South Carolina, in 1838, his passionate refusal to surrender rallied the Seminoles. He became a symbol of Indian resistance comparable to such great figures in American history as Tecumseh of the Shawnee and Crazy Horse of the Lakota Sioux.

$\mathbf{A}$mong the great Seminole leaders was Billy Bowlegs, who posed for this daguerreotype, an early type of photograph, while visiting New York in 1852.

The bloodiest battle of the Second Seminole War took place in a swamp on the north shore of Lake Okeechobee on December 25, 1837, when United States troops engaged a band of Seminole warriors. Twenty-six of the thirty-seven dead were American soldiers. By making surprise attacks and then melting back into the thick green foliage, often in heat and humidity that the soldiers found intolerable, several hundred Seminoles eluded capture by the more than 40,000 United States regulars and volunteers who served during the seven years of this war.

Although his exploits have not been highly publicized, Seminole medicine man Arpeika was as important to the war as the legendary Osceola. He inspired warriors to fight fiercely for their freedom in several battles, including the Battle of Okeechobee. Even when surrounded, Arpeika refused a flag of truce and entertained no thought of compromise with the invading forces. The only Seminole leader to remain in Florida, he made his last camp in Big Cypress Swamp, not far from the present-day Seminole community.

African Americans made up about a quarter of the fighting force in the Second Seminole War, just as they did in the first. Afterward, some of the blacks moved to Indian Territory. Others escaped to Mexico or were returned to former slaveholders. They proved that they could not only fight valiantly for their freedom, but could demonstrate leadership qualities in battle. Their participation both inflamed the controversy and greatly strengthened the Seminoles in their battle for survival.

On May 10, 1842, a frustrated President John Tyler ordered the end of military actions against the Seminoles—despite the fact that millions of dollars had been spent, fifteen hundred American soldiers had died, and no peace treaty had been signed. However, more than three thousand Seminoles were among those removed to Oklahoma. Many died along the way; others survived the arduous journey, and their descendants live there to this day as members of the Seminole Nation of Oklahoma. Yet a small number of Seminoles proudly continued to hold out in the Florida swamps, refusing to sign any peace treaty with the United States.

Just thirteen years later, a party of army surveyors was attacked by warriors under the command of the colorful leader Billy Bowlegs. This led to the Third Seminole War, which lasted from 1855 to 1858. The United States again made an all-out effort and finally captured and relocated Bowlegs, so bringing to a close the long conflict between the Seminoles and the United States. On May 4, 1858, the United States declared an end to hostilities in the third war, but no peace treaty has ever been signed. These three wars cost over $20 million and the lives of many American soldiers. Many Seminoles were also killed or exiled. By the end of the Seminole Wars, over 4,000 men, women, and children had been forcibly moved west of the Mississippi River. However, several hundred unconquered men, women, and children—estimates range from 150 to 550—still hid in the Everglades of south Florida. Nothing, including offers of land and cattle, could persuade these wary people to emerge from the wilderness. Little was seen of them for two decades, until late in the century when trading posts were opened at Fort Lauderdale, Chokoloskee, and elsewhere, and a few Seminoles came out of hiding to trade with the newcomers.

After the Florida Wars

The unconquered Seminoles belonged to at least two major groups. Muskogee-speaking people lived near Lake Okeechobee; those who spoke the related Miccosukee tongue made their home to the south and preferred to be called Miccosukee. These groups sustained themselves by raising a few pigs, chickens, cattle, and small crops of fruits and vegetables, along with hunting, trapping, fishing, and gathering in the wilds around them. Hearts of palm, also known as swamp cabbage, was a vital food. They lived isolat-

Dressed in a blend of traditional and Western clothing, this group of men was photographed around 1900—a time when the Florida Seminoles were undergoing many changes.

Many Seminoles continue to live near the Everglades. They have long appreciated the water and the wildlife of this vast wetland, and hope that it can be saved for future generations.

ed from the rest of the world in the remote, unexplored wetlands until well into the twentieth century. Their descendants eventually became the Seminole Tribe of Florida, the Miccosukee Tribe of Indians of Florida, and the unaffiliated Independent, or Traditional, Seminoles of the present day.

Finally at peace with the United States, the Seminoles entered the twentieth century in the same condition as they were in at the conclusion of the Seminole Wars—living in poverty in the swampy wilderness of south Florida. Through the first half of the century, many subsisted by means of seasonal farmwork, craft sales to tourists, and alligator wrestling. Others still secreted themselves in the backwaters of the Everglades. They distrusted the government, preferring to live on their own, as long as they could provide for their families. However, as the coastal rivers and plains came to be settled, developers and politicians sought to drain the Everglades. The damaged environment drastically reduced the fish and game upon which the Seminoles depended. Droughts and hurricanes also led to poor crops. Living at the edge of survival, by the 1920s the Seminoles were nearly forced to abandon their way of life. They were threatened with a choice between extinction or assimilation with the dominant American population.

However, in 1934, recognizing the plight of Native American people, the United States Congress passed the Indian Reorganization Act. This law granted American Indians the right to conduct popular elections and govern themselves according to their own constitutions and bylaws. In 1938, Congress set aside over 80,000 acres of land in Florida for the Seminoles in the Big Cypress Swamp, Brighton, and Hollywood. The Seminoles were encouraged to give up their lifeways in favor of larger-scale agriculture. However, the Seminoles still mistrusted the government that had waged war against their grandfathers. Even religious missionaries were unable to break the Seminole spirit of independence.

In 1947, the Seminoles filed a petition with the United States Indian Claims Commission for the return of land taken by the government. In the late 1950s after federal legislation granted more rights to Indian reservations, a new generation of Seminole leaders, the children of the last generation to hide in the swamps, began to meet regularly beneath a huge oak tree on the Hollywood Reservation. Called the Council Oak, the tree is still standing—it was spared during the construction of a parking lot near the corner of U.S. Highway 441 and Stirling Road on the reservation. Leaders envisioned that a constitutional form of government would bring greater independence and economic opportunity to the Seminole people.

By 1957, after many open meetings, a constitution was drafted. It called for two layers of government—a Tribal Council and a Board of Directors—with elected representatives from each community. On July 21, 1957, tribal members voted in favor of a constitution that established the Seminole Tribe of Florida. The same year Congress officially recognized the Seminole Tribe of Florida, which soon became embroiled in the turmoil of the federal bureaucracy that oversaw Native American affairs. During this time, the Miccosukee Tribe sought recognition as a separate people; this was granted in 1962. Several dozen Florida natives not enrolled in either tribe are today considered Independent, that is, not formally recognized by the Bureau of Indian Affairs. They continue to oppose any governmental intrusion in their lives and to claim much of the land that is now the state of Florida.

The first Seminole government forged a unified organization and raised funds for a modest treasury, thus initiating the modern era of the Seminole Tribe of Florida. The framers of the tribal constitution envisioned prosperity far exceeding the small profits from alligator wrestling shows, airboat rides, roadside arts and crafts booths, and village tours. Over time their efforts have brought economic stability to the tribe and security to its members. In 1970, the Indian Claims Commission awarded the Seminole of Oklahoma and Florida $12,347,500 for the land taken from them by the United States. In 1992, the tribe was also finally awarded a settlement on the land claim filed in 1947.

The next generation of leaders, including Betty Mae Jumper, the first woman to be elected chair of an American Indian tribe, competently guided the reservation on several business ventures that brought considerable wealth to the Seminoles. In 1977, the opening of the first "smoke shop," which offered discount, tax-free tobacco products, brought in enough revenue to sustain the tribe. The opening of a bingo hall in Hollywood, Florida, shortly after community activist James Billie's election as Tribal Council chair, was the first on any reservation in the United States. Under Billie's leadership the Seminole Tribe of Florida has grown dramatically—both politically and financially.

The establishment of two new reservations, at Tampa and Immokalee, has increased Seminole land holdings in Florida to over 90,000 acres. The opening of a new hotel in Tampa, a venture into the citrus market, the founding of the Ahfachkee Indian School, the creation of the Ah-Tah-Thi-Ki Museum and the Billie Swamp Safari, and the expansion of the profitable smoke shops and gaming enterprises have all contributed to making the Seminoles financially independent.

6. New Ways

The Seminole way of life has changed dramatically over the years. Here, a woman makes dolls, which she will sell to tourists, a constant presence in Florida's sprawling wetlands.

MOST TRIBAL MEMBERS NOW HAVE MODERN HOUSING AND ACCESS TO health care. The tribe spends over $1 million annually on education; this includes supporting the Ahfachkee Indian School and supplying financial aid to college students. The Seminole Tribe employs more than three hundred members, quite a few of whom work in legal and law enforcement departments. Many new enterprises are supported by the Tribal Council and Board.

As established in the constitution, the Tribal Council is the governing body of the Seminole Tribe of Florida. It is composed of a chairperson, a vice-chair, and council representatives from each reservation. Today, the council administers the tribe's enterprises, as well as water resource management and utilities departments. The Seminole Tribe of Florida itself is exempt from all federal and state taxes, although individual members are responsible for the same state and federal taxes as other American citizens. The tribe does not have a court system—legal matters not resolved on the community level are referred to the proper state or federal authorities. However, the Seminole Tribe has a public defender's office, which provides legal services to tribal members. Bullets no longer whiz past the descendants of Osceola, Jumper, Micanopy, and Sam Jones as they fight for survival. The battleground is now the courtroom, where the unconquered Seminoles continue to fight vigorously for their rights as a people.

Today, the Seminoles of Florida proudly refer to themselves as the Unconquered People. Descendants of a small band of just three hundred people, they skillfully outwitted the powerful

*P*eople once glided through the Everglades in dugout canoes. Today, the graceful dugouts are still produced in a few remote places, but for the most part, boatbuilding has become a lost art.

*S*eminole men continue to practice the art of wood carving. They make and sell small canoes, tomahawks, and knives.

Seminole women are known far and wide for their long cotton dresses. Each of the colorful dresses is highly adorned with patchwork, often in a geometric design.

Sometimes, women sew delicate rows of beads in distinctive patterns on their dresses. Whatever their design, the dresses express the Seminole love of bright colors and original patterns.

forces of the United States Army in the nineteenth century. Their number has now grown to over two thousand people in south Florida. The Seminole Tribe of Florida exists only because the Seminole people refused to be destroyed or scattered. Instead they have reshaped their culture to keep many of the old ways while adapting to contemporary life. A few continue to live in chickees. Some wear clothing that has evolved into a distinctive style, and many, like their ancestors, honor the passing of the seasons. They also share their culture by performing traditional dance and music for young people in schools across the state.

Seminole Language

Most of the Creek peoples spoke various dialects of Muskogee, also known as Muscogee or Creek. The most common language of the Southeast Indians, it included the dialects of the Chickasaw and the Choctaw. As descendants of Creek bands, many Seminoles speak Muskogee, though some bands speak the Miccosukee, or Mikasuki, dialect. The Seminole Tribe of Florida has traditionally included both Muskogean- and Miccosukee-speaking people. However, in 1962, a new tribal organization was formed, and many Florida Indians previously considered Seminoles now call themselves the Miccosukee Tribe of Indians of Florida. To further complicate the situation, many Independents don't wish to belong to either tribe, preferring to be known simply as Seminoles.

In any case, the Seminoles have two languages, both unwritten, which are still spoken today. Muskogee and Miccosukee are related, although speakers cannot understand each other. Some words in the two languages are similar while others are completely different. Many Seminoles are fluent in both languages, while others speak only Muskogee or Miccosukee.

The names of many Florida cities, counties, places, rivers, and lakes are drawn from Seminole words, both Muskogee and Miccosukee. Here are some examples from the website of the Seminole Tribe of Florida:

Apalachicola	place of the ruling people
Chattahoochee	marked stones
Hialeah	prairie
Homosassa	pepper place
Immokalee	my camp
Miami	that place
Ocala	spring
Okeechobee	big water
Pahokee	grassy water
Palatka	ferry crossing
Thonotosassa	flint place
Yeehaw	wolf

Both languages have sounds and complex sentence structures not found in English, which makes them difficult for non-native speakers. Here are a few words written phonetically that you might like to try:

chen-te	snake
coo-wah-chobee	big cat
ee-cho	deer
hen-le	squirrel
ke-hay-ke	hawk
laa-le	fish
nak-ne	man
o-pa	owl
sho-ke	pig
ya-laahe	orange
yok-che	turtle

The Seminole Nation of Oklahoma

Uprooted from their ancestral homes in the 1830s, many Seminoles, including people of mixed blood, marched under military escort into the harsh wilderness of Indian Territory. They demonstrated great courage and ability as they went to work making a new home for themselves in the rugged, unfamiliar landscape. For nearly twenty years after relocation, they were forced to live with the Creeks, who came to be known as the Muskogee Creeks. Finally, in 1856, a treaty was made with the Muskogee

Creeks and the federal government that permitted a separate Seminole Nation to be established in Oklahoma. Living in the first independent nation within the United States, the Oklahoma Seminoles were granted land north of the Canadian River. This land was bounded on the east by a line marked by the present-day city of Tecumseh and on the west by the one hundredth meridian, which was then the western border of the United States.

Under the leadership of Chief John Jumper, the Seminoles established a capital known as the Green Head Prairie. Then came the Civil War, and all the native people of Oklahoma became bitterly divided. The Seminoles fought each other, and as they also engaged in war with factions of Cherokee, Choctaw, and other tribes that had been removed to Oklahoma from the Southeast, the territory became a bloody land. About one-third of the Seminoles, under the leadership of Big John Chupco, remained loyal to the Union and moved to Kansas. However, most of the Seminoles, led by John Jumper, allied with the Confederacy. At the end of the war the Seminoles were forced to give up their land and many tribal rights. They were eventually allowed to buy land from the Muskogee Creeks, but at a high price. This land became the Second Seminole Nation from 1866 to 1907. Elijah Brown, leader of its northern faction, established a new capital in 1866 in the city of Wewoka, or Barking Water, which later became the county seat in Seminole County.

Friction continued between the northern and southern factions of the Seminoles, but over time they agreed on leaders and a form of government based upon the traditional way of life. Each band elected representatives to serve on the council. The council selected two members as candidates for chief and upon the day of election, these two candidates appeared on the main street of Wewoka. Voters lined up behind their preferred candidate, and the one with the most people in his line was elected to a four-year term as chief.

Before moving from Florida, the Seminoles had thirty-five bands, but only twenty-five remained after they were relocated to Indian Territory. Following the Civil War, the bands continued to decline, until there were only fourteen when Oklahoma became a state. Today, the Seminole Nation of Oklahoma is composed of these fourteen bands, two of which are largely freedmen bands made up of the descendants of slaves who found refuge with the Seminoles prior to their exodus from Florida. With its own elected chairman and vice-chairman, each band meets once a month to discuss tribal matters.

The Seminole Nation of Oklahoma also has an elected chief and assistant chief, who represent the entire tribe. These individuals are responsible for economic development, employment opportunities, social programs, and other administrative matters—along with the General Council, the governing body of the Seminole Nation. Consisting of two elected representatives from each band, the General Council holds quarterly meetings to discuss and decide key issues. The tribal headquarters is still in Wewoka, which today has a population of around four thousand people. Located in the farming country of central Oklahoma, Wewoka is about sixty-five miles southeast of Oklahoma City. Oil is a primary natural resource of the region and industries in Wewoka have produced oil field equipment, gasoline, chemicals, and other goods. Seminole people are scattered throughout Seminole County—one of the poorest counties of Oklahoma. The nation currently has around twelve thousand enrolled members, about 60 percent of whom live within or near the tribal boundaries. About seven hundred people live out of state, and the rest make their homes in other parts of Oklahoma.

The Seminoles of Oklahoma are a proud people, who are strongly devoted to their heritage, which is preserved in art, storytelling, music, and stomp dances. Elders are especially honored for their wisdom and knowledge of history and traditions. Both Christianity and native religion are practiced by the Oklahoma Seminoles. Native religion centers around the stomp dance, which is drawn from the Green Corn Ceremony. Older people still speak Muskogee, but the language is fading away, in part because of the influence of television and the mass media in general. However, efforts are being made to teach the language in the public schools, so the Seminole way of life may continue long into the future.

As the Everglades have changed dramatically over the years, so has the Seminole way of life. Here, the sun breaks through the clouds at dawn over one of the last stretches of undisturbed water in this sprawling wetland.

More About

Time Line

1513   The Spanish claim what is now the southeastern United States, which they call La Florida.

1539–43   Hernando DeSoto explores the Southeast, encountering many native peoples.

1670   The English found Charleston, South Carolina, and begin to skirmish with the Spanish in Atlantic coastal waters.

1701   During the War of Spanish Succession, the Creeks ally themselves with the British and invade Florida.

1704–1708   The English destroy Spanish missions in Florida, killing or enslaving thousands of native people.

1700s With the death and enslavement of Florida natives, the Creeks settle in northern Florida and become the first Seminoles.

1740   Alachua, the earliest known Seminole town in Florida, is established.

1763   Spain cedes Florida to England.

1776   The American Revolution leads to independence for the United States.

1783   Florida is returned to Spain in the Treaty of Paris.

about 1804   Osceola (William Powell) is born.

1813–1814   The Creek War in Alabama forces Indians to join natives in Florida. Andrew Jackson achieves fame as an "Indian fighter."

1817   The First Seminole War begins when General Andrew Jackson invades Florida on a military campaign.

1819   Florida is ceded to the United States and becomes a territory, ending the military campaign of the First Seminole War.

1823   In the Treaty of Moultrie Creek the Seminoles are forced to surrender 28 million acres, all but 4 million acres of their land. The treaty officially concludes the First Seminole War.

1832 In the Treaty of Payne's Landing five million acres in southwest Florida are promised to the Seminoles.

1835 The Second Seminole War (1835–1842) begins when Osceola leads warriors at the Battle of Withlacoochee, killing Major Francis Dade and over a hundred soldiers on their way to Fort King (Ocala).

1837 Osceola is captured, despite a flag of truce, and exiled to a South Carolina prison, where he dies in January 1838. On Christmas Day in the Battle of Okeechobee, fewer than five hundred Seminoles, led by Alligator, Arpeika, Jumper, and others, confront a thousand troops under General Zachary Taylor.

1838 Around 3,000 Seminoles, including Wildcat (Coacoochee) and Alligator are exiled to Oklahoma.

1855 Billy Bowlegs leads a daring attack on army surveyors, igniting the Third Seminole War.

1858 The Third Seminole War ends with the capture of Bowlegs, but several hundred Seminoles, including Arpeika, hide out in the Big Cypress Swamp and other isolated wilderness areas of Florida. The United States abandons efforts to capture and remove them.

1926 A hurricane devastates the Everglades, leaving many Seminoles homeless.

1928 The Tamiami Trail is opened, leading to a boom of tourism in south Florida. Seminoles begin to sell crafts and wrestle alligators. A deadly hurricane strikes the Lake Okeechobee region.

1934 The Indian Reorganization Act permits self-determination for American Indians.

1939 Brighton Indian Day School, offering Seminole children their first opportunity for a formal education, is opened by William and Edith Boehmer.

1946 The United States Indian Claims Commission is established.

1947 Seminole leaders file a petition with the Claims Commission for a settlement for lands taken from them. Students at Florida State

University choose "Seminoles" as their official team name.

1957 The Seminole Constitution is ratified by vote of 241 to 5, ensuring federal status for the Seminole Tribe of Florida.

1962 Miccosukee Tribe of Indians of Florida gains federal recognition.

1963 The first Seminole newspaper, *Smoke Signals*, is published. (Renamed *Alligator Times* in 1973 and *Seminole Tribune* in 1982).

1967 Betty Mae Jumper is elected chairperson of the Seminole Nation of Florida. This makes her the first woman chair of any Indian tribe in North America.

1971 Howard Tommie is elected chairperson of the Seminole Nation of Florida. During his eight-year term sale of tax-free cigarettes boosts the tribal budget to $4.5 million a year.

1979 James E. Billie is elected chairperson of the Seminole Nation of Florida. Bingo becomes the biggest source of income. The Immokalee and Tampa Reservations are established.

1992 Seminoles in Florida and Oklahoma receive a financial settlement from the United States for land taken from them during the Seminole Wars. Although the Seminole Tribe of Florida receives close to $10 million, the Independent Seminoles refuse to settle, and their funds are held in trust.

1995 The Seminole Tribe of Florida moves its headquarters to a new four-story building in Hollywood, Florida.

1996 Fort Pierce Reservation is established. Cattleman Fred Smith, the longest-serving tribal chair, dies. James Billie is elected to an unprecedented fifth term as chairperson. Tribal budget exceeds $100 million.

1997 Sovereignty of the Seminole Nation of Florida is challenged by the National Indian Gaming Commission. Seminoles assume full management of gaming activities on Hollywood Reservation. Ah-Tah-Thi-Ki Museum opens. The Seminole people of Florida mark the fortieth anniversary of the creation of their tribal government.

Notable People

Alligator (Halpatter Tustenuggee) (about 1795–1850) settled in central Florida with his Creek parents when he was a young boy. He grew up to become a great leader among the Seminoles. On December 28, 1835, Jumper, Micanopy, and Alligator led three hundred warriors against Major Francis Dade's troop of just over one hundred soldiers in the Second Seminole War. All but three of the soldiers were massacred. Three day's later, on New Year's Eve, Osceola and his warriors joined with Alligator in an attack on General Duncan Clinch's force on the Withlacoochee River. Alligator continued to battle American soldiers. The next major engagement was at Lake Okeechobee in December 1837. Here, Arpeika, Wildcat, and Alligator fought Colonel Zachary Taylor. Because of a brutal scorched-earth policy in which Seminole camps and crops were destroyed, Alligator was forced to surrender in March 1838. He escaped that year, but was recaptured and sent to Indian Territory. In 1843 he was a member of a Seminole delegation that lobbied in Washington, D.C., for better living conditions and for improved relations between Creeks and Seminoles.

Arpeika (Aripeka, Apayaka Hadjo, Sam Jones) (about 1765–1860) most likely was born in Georgia and moved to Florida with other Miccosukee people. A medicine man and war chief, he headed a village north of Tampa, where the town of Arpeika stands today; he later (by 1841) was in charge of a village north of Lake Okeechobee.

Along with Osceola, Wildcat, and Alligator, Arpeika fiercely resisted Seminole removal from Florida. He advised Osceola to seek vengeance against Indian agent Wiley Thompson, triggering war with the Americans in 1835. Always distrustful of the settlers and soldiers, he fought alongside Wildcat and Alligator in a major battle at Lake Okeechobee in December 1837. Both the American soldiers and the

Seminoles sustained heavy losses, but Arpeika and his band were never defeated and never relocated.

During the Third Seminole War of 1855–1858, Arpeika, along with Billy Bowlegs, continued to battle American forces. Even after Billy Bowlegs decided to migrate to Indian Territory, Arpeika remained in the Florida Everglades. He died soon after the end of hostilities. His exact age was never known; he could have been over 100 years old.

Bolek (Boleck, Bowlegs) (active early 1800s) was a Seminole leader who fought United States forces along the border between Georgia and Florida in 1812. Living in a village on the Suwanee River in western Florida, he allied with his brother, King Payne, to prevent Georgians from pursuing and capturing runaway slaves. During a skirmish with Georgia militia, King Payne was killed and Bolek was wounded. Upon the death of his brother, Bolek became principal chief.

In the First Seminole War of 1817–1818, American soldiers under the command of General Andrew Jackson invaded Florida, which was under Spanish colonial rule. He attacked several settlements, including Bolek's village, which was already abandoned. A year later, in 1819, Florida was sold to the United States.

Bolek died not long after the United States assumed control of Florida. At his death, Micanopy, the grandson of King Payne, assumed his leadership position.

Billy Bowlegs (Holata Mico) (about 1810–1864), a prominent war chief, led one of the last Seminole bands to remain in Florida. Born on Alachua Savannah, the present site of Cuscowilla, Florida, he was also known as Halpuda Mikko, meaning "alligator chief." During the Second Seminole War of 1835–1842, he took part in several battles along with other Seminole leaders. A year after the death of Osceola, he attacked a trading post opened on Seminole land by Colonel

William S. Harney. For nearly a year, his band hid out in the Everglades, evading soldiers during the day and raiding at night. Exhausted and near starvation, he and his party finally surrendered in 1842, but they refused to move to Indian Territory. He was given a small parcel of land in Florida.

Hostilities broke out again in 1855, when army engineers and surveyors stole crops and cut down banana trees owned by Bowleg's group. In retaliation, Bowlegs led his warriors in a number of raids against settlers and traders. This marked the beginning of the Third Seminole War. Again, soldiers could not defeat the skillful Bowlegs and his band. Finally, in 1858, a group of Seminoles were brought back from Indian Territory to negotiate a peace settlement that included a large cash payment. Bowlegs and some of his people agreed to move to Indian Territory; others joined Arpeika's band which refused to leave Florida. With his band of thirty-three warriors and eighty women, Bowlegs moved to lands on the north and south forks of the Canadian River in Indian Territory. He fought for the Union under Opothleyaholo during the American Civil War.

Foke Luste Hajo

Foke Luste Hajo (Foke-Lustee Hadjo, Fuche Luste Hadjo, Black Dirt) (active 1830s) signed the Treaty of Payne's Landing in 1832, along with Charley Emathla, and the Treaty of Fort Gibson in 1833, in which the

Seminoles agreed to move from Florida to Indian Territory. The signings infuriated Seminoles who sided with Osceola and opposed removal. Two years later, in 1835, Osceola and many other Seminoles decided to fight relocation and they killed Emathla. Fearing for their lives, Foke Luste Hajo and his followers fled to Fort Brooke at the present-day site of Tampa, where they were protected by American military forces. They were later moved to Indian Territory.

Josiah Francis (active 1810s) was a medicine man and spiritual leader in the Creek War of 1813–1814 and the First Seminole War. Of mixed Creek, Seminole, and Anglo ancestry, he is believed to have been related to one of the Alabama tribes, perhaps the Tuskegee or Tawasa. However, he is most closely associated with the Red Stick Creeks and the Seminoles. A friend of Tecumseh, he traveled with the famous Native American leader in 1811 to forge an alliance of many tribes.

Among the Seminoles, he was known as Francis the Prophet during the battles against General Andrew Jackson. In 1815, Francis journeyed to England to seek help in fighting the Americans who were pushing into Creek and Seminole lands. In 1817, his daughter Milly pleaded with him to stop the execution of Duncan McKrimmon, a Georgia militiaman, and Francis spared the man's life. A year later in 1818, on the Saint Marks River, Francis was lured by Americans onto a gunboat flying a British flag. After his capture, Andrew Jackson ordered his execution.

Milly Hayo Francis (1802–1848) begged her father to spare the life of Duncan McKrimmon, as the officer in the Georgia militia was about to be burned at the stake. Her father ignored her pleas until she offered to be burned at the stake along with McKrimmon. The militiaman was released upon condition that he shave his head and live among the Seminoles.

Just months later, Milly's father was captured and killed. As the war was ending, Milly was near starvation, and she traveled with her mother and sister to an army post to ask for food. McKrimmon, who had returned from captivity, was now stationed at the fort. He is credited with giving her food and thereby saving her life, just as she had once rescued him. He also asked Milly to marry him, but she refused, thinking he was doing so only out of gratitude for her saving her life. Remaining with her people, she later moved to Indian Territory, settling near Muskogee, Oklahoma. Because of her conduct in the First Seminole War, she was awarded a small pension by the United States in 1844. However, payment was delayed, and she died of tuberculosis four years later without receiving any of the promised assistance.

Jumper (Ote Emathla, Otee Amathla) (about 1790–1838) took part in the Creek War of 1813–1814 as a member of the Red Stick Creeks, after which he settled in Florida. His Indian name means "he makes sense." Jumper fought against General Andrew Jackson in the First Seminole War. In the 1830s during the Second Seminole War, he strongly opposed removal to Indian Territory. As Micanopy's adviser, he participated in the attack on Francis Dade's troops in December 1835. Later, he and other Seminoles joined Osceola to attack a group of soldiers under the command of General Duncan L. Clinch. After Jumper surrendered in 1837, he was sent west to Indian Territory, but died along the way in 1838. His son Jim Jumper was elected principal chief of the Western Seminoles in Indian Territory in 1848.

Betty Mae Tiger Jumper (1923–   ), a nurse, leader, journalist, and storyteller, was born in Indiantown, a little village in the Everglades. Her father was of European descent and her mother was a Seminole who spoke little English. Betty Mae and her younger brother grew up in a traditional Seminole home, although she attended day school and later a boarding school in Cherokee, North Carolina. In 1945, she became the first Seminole to graduate from high school.

She moved to Oklahoma where she studied to become the first Seminole nurse. When she returned to Florida, she married Moses Jumper. Through the 1950s, she worked diligently to improve health services on the reservations. When the Seminole Tribe of Florida was formed in 1957, she became a representative and later a board member, and in 1967 she was elected the tribe's second chairperson. She continued to work in tribal administration through the 1960s; then in 1971 she became director of operations for Seminole Communications, which publishes the *Seminole Tribune*, a highly respected biweekly newspaper. In recent years, Betty Mae has become an accomplished storyteller and public speaker about the history and culture of the Seminoles. The author of *Legends of the Seminoles*, she often recounts stories remembered from her childhood at the annual Florida Folk Festival and other events.

John Jumper (Hemha Micco, Otee Emathla) (about 1820–1896) was born and raised in Florida. However, he was forced to move to Indian Territory in 1840. As a young man he took part in battles against removal. However, despite his strength and size (he stood six feet, four inches tall and weighed over two hundred pounds), he consistently advocated peace with the government. In 1856, the Seminoles finally formed a distinct nation separate from the Creeks in Oklahoma. In 1861, along with Cherokee leader Stand Watie, John Jumper supported the Confederacy in the Civil War. They forced Indians who supported the Union cause to move to Kansas, but were defeated by Union troops under General James G. Blunt. After the war, Jumper devoted himself to protecting Seminole lands in Oklahoma. A devout Christian, he became pastor of the Spring Baptist Church in 1877. He was elected chief of the Western Seminoles in 1881. He remained chief and pastor until 1894 and died two years later.

Kinache (about 1750–1819) sided with the British during the American Revolution. At that time he was living just above the forks of the Apalachicola River. After the war, in 1783, he moved to a Miccosukee village in Florida on the western shore of Lake Miccosukee. (Between 1800 to 1802, Bolek also used Lake Miccosukee as a base.) Among his many other names, Kinache was known as Lye Drop Mico, which means "far-off warrior." He allied himself with the British during the War of 1812, and it is believed that he fought against General Andrew Jackson in the Battle of New Orleans in 1815. A year later, he helped to defend Fort Negro (later Fort Gadsden) against an attack by American troops who were pursuing runaway slaves. In 1818, a band of Creeks under the command of William McIntosh attacked the Miccosukees. It was reported that Kinache was killed in the engagement, but he escaped to the Bahamas, and returned to Florida in 1819. He died later that year.

Micanopy (Micco-Nuppe, Michenopah) (about 1780–1849) was probably born near Saint Augustine, Florida. He was the grandson of King Payne, the grandnephew of Bolek, and the uncle of Wildcat. His Seminole name means "head chief." He was sometimes called Halputta Hadjo, or "crazy alligator." He became a prominent Seminole leader at the death of Bolek, who had succeeded King Payne. Over the years, he acquired considerable land, livestock, and slaves.

Micanopy

When a number of Seminole leaders agreed in the Treaty of Payne's Landing to give up their land and move to Indian Territory in 1832, Micanopy refused to sign the document. He worked to live peacefully with the Americans, but he also supported young warriors, including Wildcat, Alligator, and Osceola, who planned to resist any attempts at removal. In December 1835, Micanopy took part in attacks on troops commanded by Major Francis Dade and General Duncan Clinch. In June 1837, the aging Micanopy decided to give up and move to Indian Territory, but Osceola kidnapped him in hopes of preventing his surrender. Later that year, Micanopy was captured under a flag of truce and sent to prison in Charleston, South Carolina. But he was allowed to emigrate to Indian Territory with about two hundred other Seminoles. He was one of the signers of the agreement that granted independence to the Western Seminoles from the Creeks. Four years later, in 1849, Micanopy died in his home in Indian Territory.

Neamathla

Neamathla (Nehe Marthla, Neah Emarthla, Innemathla) (active 1820s) was of Creek descent, but he achieved fame as a leader of the Miccosukee, a branch of the Seminole. In 1817, he demanded that settlers end their encroachment on the land of his people. In retaliation, American troops from Fort Scott, Georgia, commanded by General Edmund Gaines, destroyed his village of Fowltown in the Florida Panhandle during the First Seminole War.

At the end of the war, Neamathla moved to an area near Tallahassee and was named principal chief of the Seminoles by government officials in 1821. However, most of the

Seminoles considered Micanopy to be their leader. In 1823, Neamathla was one of the signers of the Treaty of Moultrie Creek in which the Seminoles gave up millions of acres of land. However, in 1826, believing that Seminoles should educate their children themselves, he refused a payment of one thousand dollars from the U.S. government to build a school. A skillful and persuasive speaker, he also encouraged Seminoles to oppose relocation. Government officials subsequently deposed him as chief, and he moved to Hatchechubbee Creek in Alabama. There he joined the Creek tribal council and fought removal, attacking settlers and stagecoaches. Alabama militiamen captured him in 1836, and he was sent to Indian Territory in shackles.

Osceola (William Powell) (about 1804–1838), the renowned Seminole warrior, was probably born on the Talapoosa River near the border of present-day Georgia and Alabama. His Seminole name was Asi-vaholo, meaning "black drink crier." His paternal grandfather is believed to have been of Scottish or English descent, although Osceola insisted that he was a full-blooded Seminole. He considered William Powell, his mother's husband, to be his stepfather.

When he was still a boy, Osceola moved to Florida with his mother and settled along the Apalachicola River. As a young man, he fought in the First Seminole War. Although Osceola was not a chief by birth, his abilities as warrior and leader were soon recognized by his people. He rose in prominence in 1835 during the Second Seminole War, which resulted from an attempt by the United States to force the Seminoles to leave their homeland in northern Florida.

Osceola rejected government treaties that called for his people to move to Indian Territory in Oklahoma. In November 1835 he killed Charley Emathla, who had agreed to removal and was preparing to leave for Indian Territory. On December 28, 1835, Osceola and his band ambushed Indian agent Wiley Thompson, who had negotiated a treaty of removal the previous year, thus precipitating the Second

Seminole War. Working from isolated camps deep in the Everglades, Osceola waged a stunning guerrilla war against superior military forces for two years. The heat and humidity, along with the thick, swampy backcountry and the shrewd tactics of the Seminoles, thwarted several army commanders. Finally, General Joseph M. Hernandez, at the order from General Thomas S. Jesup, captured him. Osceola was imprisoned at Saint Augustine, Florida, and later transferred to Fort Moultrie in the harbor of Charleston, South Carolina. A prisoner of war, he died there on January 30, 1838. Osceola's people valiantly struggled until 1842, when all but a few hundred people were forced to march west to Oklahoma.

Payne (King Payne) (active 1800–1812) was principal chief when Creek and Seminole bands from northern Florida raided American settlements in Georgia in the early 1800s. The warriors were encouraged by the Spanish, who thought the tribes might serve as a buffer to American encroachment. In retaliation, a force of Georgia militia drove a hundred miles into Spanish Florida to attack the Seminoles in 1812. In one of these engagements, Payne, who was known by the settlers as King Payne, was killed and his brother Bolek was wounded. However, the troops were driven back. The following year Colonel John Williams and a force of U.S. soldiers and Tennessee militiamen invaded Florida, burning Seminole villages, destroying crops, and seizing livestock. These border battles led to the Creek War of 1813–14 and the First Seminole War of 1817–1819.

Jerome Richard Tiger (Kocha) (1941–1967) was a promising young artist whose career was ended prematurely when he died at the age of twenty-six. Born at Tahlequah, Oklahoma, he was the son of Reverend John M. Tiger (Seminole) and Lucinda Lewis (Creek). He attended public schools in Muskogee and Eufaula, then attended the Cleveland Engineering Institute for one year. He served two years in the United

States Naval Reserves from 1958 to 1960, and married Margaret (Peggy) Lois Raymond in 1960. They had three children. In 1962, he began to paint and he sent several of his works to a major competition–the Philbrook Indian Art Annual. His paintings received acclaim for their precision and strong colors, as well as the delicacy of their style. His works dealt with both traditional subjects and mythology. Highly prized, his paintings were eagerly sought by collectors. On August 13, 1967, he accidentally killed himself with a revolver.

Jerome Richard Tiger

Wildcat (Wild Cat, Coacoochee, Cowacoochee) (about 1810–1857) was born in the village of Yulaka along the Saint Johns River in northern Florida. It was said that he had a twin sister who died at birth. Being a twin was believed to give him special powers. The nephew of Micanopy, he grew up to become a great leader. When he was just nineteen, Wildcat led a band of Seminole warriors and runaway slaves in the Second Seminole War. His father, Emathla, was captured and imprisoned at Fort Marion in 1837.

In October of that year, Wildcat emerged from the swamp with a pipe from Osceola decorated with a white feather of peace. However, during the meeting with General Thomas Jesup, the Seminoles, including Osceola and Wildcat, were arrested, despite the flag of truce. Wildcat and his followers fasted for six days, then managed to escape from Fort Marion.

Wildcat led several raids to avenge his betrayal. On Christmas Day, 1837, he joined with Alligator and Arpeika in the Battle of Lake

Okeechobee. Although the soldiers under Colonel Zachary Taylor held their ground, the Seminole warriors inflicted great casualties on them before vanishing back into the Everglades. Wildcat held on for two more years before he and his followers, exhausted and starving, agreed to be relocated.

In 1843, Alligator and Wildcat went to Washington, D.C., as tribal delegates seeking financial assistance for their people. Although the Western Seminole lived in deep poverty, their request was denied. In 1849, Wildcat and about a hundred of his warriors went to Texas where they were joined by about a thousand Kickapoos. They attempted to establish a new community, and the Mexican government eventually granted them some land. Wildcat became a colonel in the Mexican army and campaigned against the Comanches and the Apaches. He died of smallpox in Mexico in 1857.

Glossary

black drink An herbal beverage used by Seminoles and other tribes of the Southeast for purification during the Green Corn and other ceremonies

breechcloth A cloth or skin worn between the legs (also breechclout)

buckskin Deer hide softened by a tanning or curing process

chickee Traditional Seminole dwelling built on a raised platform with open sides and a thatched roof

clan Members of a large family group who trace their descent from a common ancestor

Everglades A vast wetland encompassing a large portion of southern Florida

Green Corn Ceremony Most important Seminole celebration of thanksgiving, forgiveness, and purification, held each year when the corn has ripened

hammock A small island of relatively dry land rising just above the swamps of southern Florida (also hummock)

Indian agent An official appointed by the Bureau of Indian Affairs to supervise government programs on a reservation or a certain region

Indian Removal Act An 1830 law that authorized the relocation of all Native Americans living in the East to Indian Territory in present-day Oklahoma

matrilineal Tracing descent through the mother's side of the family

medicine bundle A small pouch holding the sacred objects used by medicine men in rituals

Miccosukee One of the branches of the Seminoles in Florida, most of whom live along the Tamiami Trail; now a federally recognized tribe

Mikasuki One of the Muskogean languages spoken by the Seminoles in Florida (also spelled Miccosukee)

Muskogean Group of related languages spoken by the majority of Native American peoples living in the Southeast (also Muskhogean)

Muskogee One of the Muskogean languages, sometimes spelled Muscogee (also called Creek), spoken by the Seminoles in Florida

Seminoles Native American people, largely of Creek descent, who settled in Florida; many were later forced to relocate to Oklahoma

sofki A popular corn drink of the southeastern Indians, including the Seminoles

Further Information

Readings

To learn more about native peoples of Florida, you may wish to read the following books, which were quite helpful in researching and writing *The Seminole*. The two stories in this book were adapted from *Creek Seminole Spirit Tales: Tribal Folklore, Legend and Myth*, compiled by Jack Gregory and Rennard Strickland.

Covington, James Warren. *The Seminoles of Florida*. Gainesville: University Press of Florida, 1993.

Downs, Dorothy. *Art of the Florida Seminole and Miccosukee Indians*. Gainesville: University Press of Florida, 1995.

Foreman, Grant. *The Five Civilized Tribes: Cherokee, Chickasaw, Choctaw, Creek, Seminole*. Norman: University of Oklahoma Press, 1977.

Howard, James Henri, and Willie Lena. *Oklahoma Seminoles: Medicines, Magic, and Religion*. Norman: University of Oklahoma Press, 1984.

Jumper, Betty Mae. *Legends of the Seminoles*. Sarasota, Fla.: Pineapple Press, 1994.

Kersey, Harry A. *Pelts, Plumes, and Hides: White Traders Among the Seminole Indians*. Gainesville: University Press of Florida, 1975.

Lantz, Raymond C. *Seminole Indians of Florida*. Bowie, Md.: Heritage Books, 1994.

MacCauley, Clay. *The Seminole Indians of Florida*. Washington, D.C.: Smithsonian Institution, Bureau of Ethnology, 1992.

Mahon, John K. *History of the Second Seminole War, 1835–1842*. Gainesville: University Press of Florida, 1991.

McReynolds, Edwin C. *The Seminoles*. Norman: University of Oklahoma Press, 1957.

Peters, Virginia Bergman. *The Florida Wars*. Hamden, Conn.: Archon Books, 1979.

Polvay, Marina. *Seminole Indian Recipes*. Surfside, Fla.: Surfside, 1987.

Porter, Kenneth Wiggins. *The Black Seminoles: History of a Freedom-Seeking People*. Gainesville: University Press of Florida, 1996.

Spoehr, Alexander. *Camp, Clan, and Kin Among the Cow Creek Seminole of Florida*. Chicago: Chicago Natural History Museum, 1941.

Spoehr, Alexander. *The Florida Seminole Camp*. New York: Kraus Reprint Company, 1968.

West, Patsy. *The Enduring Seminoles: From Alligator Wrestling to Ecotourism*. Gainesville: University Press of Florida, 1998.

Young readers may find the following books to be of particular interest:

Andryszewski, Tricia. *The Seminoles: People of the Southeast*. Brookfield, Conn.: Millbrook Press, 1995.

Bland, Celia. *Osceola: Seminole Rebel*. New York: Chelsea House, 1994.

Brooks, Barbara. *The Seminole*. Vero Beach, Fla.: Rourke, 1989.

Garbarino, Merwyn S. *The Seminole*. New York: Chelsea House, 1989.

Jones, Kenneth M. *War with the Seminoles: 1835–1842: The Florida Indians Fight for Their Freedom and Homeland*. New York.: Franklin Watts, 1975.

Jumper, Moses. *Osceola, Patriot and Warrior*. Austin, Tex.: Raintree Steck-Vaughn, 1993.

Koslow, Philip. *The Seminole Indians*. New York: Chelsea Juniors, 1994.

Lee, Martin. *The Seminoles*. New York: Franklin Watts, 1989.

Lepthien, Emilie U. *The Seminole*. Chicago: Childrens Press, 1985.

Lund, Bill. *The Seminole Indians*. Mankato, Minn.: Bridgestone Books, 1997.

Neill, Wilfred T. *The Story of Florida's Seminole Indians*. St. Petersburg, Fla.: Great Outdoors, 1976.

Sanford, William R. *Osceola: Seminole Warrior*. Hillside, N.J.: Enslow, 1994.

Sneve, Virginia Driving Hawk. *The Seminoles*. New York: Holiday House, 1994.

Syme, Ronald. *Osceola, Seminole Leader*. New York: Morrow, 1976.

Weisman, Brent Richards. *Unconquered People: Florida's Seminole and Miccosukee Indians*. Gainesville: University Press of Florida, 1999.

Websites

Over the past few years, Native Americans have established themselves on the Internet. Here are some of the best and most interesting websites to visit for more information about the Seminole people, several of which were consulted in the research for this book. The website of the Seminole Tribe of Florida is highly recommended.

Florida Department of State (Seminoles)
http://www.dos.state.fl.us/flafacts/seminole.html

Florida of the Seminoles
http://www.hcc.cc.fl.us/services/faculty/bobleonard/history/seminol.htm

Second Seminole War
http://www.starbanner.com/History/SecondSeminoleWar.html

Seminole Literature
http://www.indians.org/welker/seminole.htm

Seminole Nation of Oklahoma
http://www.cowboy.net/native/seminole/index.html

Seminole Nation Museum
http://www.wewoka.com/seminole.htm

Seminole Tribe of Florida
http://www.seminoletribe.com/

Seminoles (Ocala Star-Banner)
http://www.starbanner.com/History/Seminoles.html
The Unconquered Seminoles
http://www.abfla.com/1tocf/seminole/semhistory.html

Organizations

If you'd like to learn more about the Seminoles, you may wish to contact or visit the following tribal offices, museums, and other organizations that serve the Seminole people:

Ah-Tah-Thi-Ki Museum
HC-61, Box 21-A
Clewiston, FL 33440
(941) 902-1113

Miccosukee Business Committee
P.O. Box 440021
Tamiami Station
Miami, FL 33144
(305) 223-8380
Fax (305) 223-1011

Native Village
3551 N. State Road 7 (441)
Hollywood, FL 33021
(954) 961-4519
Fax (954) 452-2745

Seminole Nation Museum
U.S. 270 & SR 56
Wewoka, OK 74884
(405) 257-5580

Seminole Nation of Oklahoma
P.O. Box 1498
Wewoka, OK 74884
(405) 257-6343
Fax (405) 257-6748

Seminole Tribe
6073 Stirling Road
Hollywood, FL 33024
(305) 321-1000
Fax (305) 581-8917

Index

Page numbers for illustrations are in **boldface**.

Raymond Bial

HAS PUBLISHED OVER THIRTY CRITICALLY ACCLAIMED BOOKS OF PHOTOGRAPHS for children and adults. His photo-essays for children include *Corn Belt Harvest, Amish Home, Frontier Home, Shaker Home, The Underground Railroad, Portrait of a Farm Family, With Needle and Thread: A Book About Quilts, Mist Over the Mountains: Appalachia and Its People, Cajun Home,* and *Where Lincoln Walked.*

He is currently immersed in writing *Lifeways,* a series of books about Native Americans. As with his other work, Bial's deep feelings for his subjects is evident in both the text and illustrations. He travels to tribal cultural centers, photographing homes, artifacts, and surroundings and learning firsthand about the national lifeways of each of these peoples.

A full-time library director at a small college in Champaign, Illinois, he lives with his wife and three children in nearby Urbana.